MY COPING SKILLS HANDBOOK

FOR 8 TO 12 YEAR OLDS

4 STEPS FOR KIDS TO C.O.P.E. WITH EVERYDAY CHALLENGES

C.O.P.E

AMANDA DOUNIS
B.SC (PSYC), B.COUN, B. TEACH, DIP. CHSP, DIP.CHILD PSYC.

WHY NOT HAVE AMANDA DOUNIS AS A GUEST SPEAKER ON YOUR PODCAST, SEMINAR OR EVENT?

POSITIVE THINKING CLINIC - SUPPORTING EMOTIONAL WELLNESS & KIDS

Email: amanda@positivethinkingclinic.com.au

Website: www.positivethinkingclinic.com.au

Facebook Group: *Emotional Wellness & Kids*

This is a callout to all Mums, Dads, Aunties, Uncles and Grandparents, make a positive impact on your children's lives with Amanda's latest book: My Coping Skills Handbook.

Amanda Dounis is the founder and operator of 4 award-winning Early Learning Centres in the St. George area of Sydney, Australia. She is the Director of the Dounis Group, and founder of The Positive Thinking Clinic.

Amanda is passionate about child development with over 20 years in the industry. She is a member of the Mental Health Academy and leading Clinical Industry Associations. She has a Bachelor of Science (Psychology), a Bachelor of Counselling and a Bachelor of Teaching, a Diploma in Professional Counselling, a Diploma in Child Psychology, and a Diploma in Clinical Hypnotherapy and Strategic Psychotherapy.

Amanda is married with two sons, volunteers for the Lifeline suicide crisis call centre and is a marathon runner.

BOOKS BY AMANDA DOUNIS

MY COPING SKILLS HANDBOOK
4 Steps for Kids to C.O.P.E. With Everyday Challenges

ONLINE COURSE BY AMANDA DOUNIS
My Coping Skills Online Course - for 8 – 12 year olds

FACEBOOK GROUP WITH AMANDA DOUNIS
Emotional Wellness & Kids

EARLY LEARNING CENTRES
https://www.stgeorgechildcare.com.au/banbury_cottage
https://www.stgeorgechildcare.com.au/little_dolphins_long_day_care_centre
https://www.stgeorgechildcare.com.au/babyland_child_care_centre
https://www.stgeorgechildcare.com.au/rainbow_cottage_child_care_centre

www.copingskillshandbook.com

MY COPING SKILLS HANDBOOK

FOR 8 TO 12 YEAR OLDS

4 STEPS FOR KIDS TO C.O.P.E. WITH EVERYDAY CHALLENGES

AMANDA DOUNIS
B.SC (PSYC), B.COUN, B. TEACH, DIP. CHSP, DIP.CHILD PSYC.

Brought to you by:
Mind Potential Publishing

Copyright © 2020 Amanda Dounis

ALL RIGHTS RESERVED. No part of this book may be reproduced or transmitted in any form whatsoever, electronic, or mechanical, including photocopying, recording, or by any informational storage or retrieval system without the expressed written permission from the author and publisher.

Author: Amanda Dounis
Title: My Coping Skills Handbook
ISBN Paperback: 978-1-922380-03-6
ISBN Kindle: 978-1-922380-05-0
Category: Self Help Techniques | Family

 A catalogue record for this book is available from the National Library of Australia

Publisher: Mind Potential Publishing
Division of Mind Design Centre Pty Ltd,
PO Box 6094, Maroochydore BC, Queensland, Australia, 4558.
International Phone: +61 405 138 567
Australia Phone: 1300 664 544
www.thepotentialist.com | www.positivethinkingclinic.com.au

Cover design by NGirl Design | www.ngirldesign.com.au

LIMITS OF LIABILITY | DISCLAIMER OF WARRANTY: The author and publisher of this book have used their best efforts in preparing this material and they disclaim any warranties, (expressed or implied) for any particular purpose. The information presented in this publication is compiled from sources believed to be accurate at the time of printing, however the publisher assumes no responsibility for omissions or errors. The author and publisher shall not be held liable for any loss or other damages, including, but not limited to incidental, consequential, or any other. This publication is not intended to replace or substitute medical or professional advice, the author and publisher disclaim any liability, loss or risk incurred as a direct or indirect consequence of the use of any content. Where real life stories are used, names have been changed to protect the privacy of individuals.

Mind Potential Publishing bears no responsibility for the accuracy of the information provided as either online or offline links contained in this publication. The use of links to websites does not constitute an endorsement by the publisher. The publisher assumes no liability for content or opinion expressed by the author. Opinions expressed by the Author do not represent the opinion of Mind Potential Publishing or Mind Design Centre Pty Ltd.

Printed in Australia

DEDICATION

"You can do anything you want darling, go and try…"

These words were spoken with love by my wonderful mother over 30 years ago. They connected deeply with my heart and mind and helped lay the foundation for a life-changing belief that I can.

So, I dedicate this book to Margaret Moraitis, my mum.

CONTENTS

Foreword	1
Introduction	3
Chapter 1: Slowing Your Busy Mind	9
Chapter 2: It's okay to win and not win	19
Chapter 3: Dealing with unkind thoughts and words	29
Chapter 4: Managing pressure and stress	41
Chapter 5: Dealing with worry	51
Chapter 6: Letting go of anger	61
Chapter 7: Moving away from sadness	73
Chapter 8: Making the most of relationships	83
Chapter 9: Cope with anything, anytime	97
Glossary of Terms	106
Acknowledgements	108
About the Contributor	111
About the Author	112

FOREWORD

This book is a great down-to-earth guide aimed to empower kids to become their own boss, develop a growth mindset and aim for their true potential.

There is evidence to show that 50 percent of mental health problems are established by age 14. This book is a powerful contribution to supporting young people to equip themselves with strategies and skills to cope with and prevent challenges from arising. It will help kids stop challenges from escalating and to keep themselves emotionally fit.

> "This book is a powerful contribution to supporting young people to equip themselves with strategies and skills to cope with and prevent challenges from arising. It will help kids stop challenges from escalating and to keep themselves emotionally fit."

Amanda has done a fabulous job of providing a real how-to guide to cope when life's challenges arrive. This book is brimming with straightforward strategies that anyone, any age, can use to reframe challenging thoughts, develop coping strategies and support themselves to choose and maintain a positive focus.

Thank you, Amanda, for your passion and commitment to supporting our next generation to be happy and mentally healthy.

Cath Shaw

Founder
Positive Living Skills Initiative Australia
A Division of PLS Learning Solutions Pty Ltd., Australasia

INTRODUCTION

Hey kids, I challenge you to be wide-eyed and curious as you read this book.

You'll learn about yourself and others, and how to cope with all kinds of challenges.

You'll discover that challenges help us learn and to adopt what I call a, growth mindset.

Growth mindset

1. Be open to learning and
2. Excited to see things from a new perspective.

Life is full of challenges. When you learn how to cope with challenges, they are the best opportunity for you to become your own expert.

You can be an expert in anything you choose.

Becoming an expert means simply that you become good at doing something you've practiced.

In this book, we're going to practice learning to cope more easily with challenges.

> Becoming an expert means simply that you become good at doing something you've practiced.

INTRODUCTION

What is a challenge?

A challenge can either be seen as positive or negative, depending on whether you have a growth mindset. Challenges can either weigh you down or make you stretch and learn something new.

We can be challenged by worry, anger, stress, friendships, chores, school work, sadness, sports, what other people think of us, and lots of other things.

> I first noticed I had those skills when my dog Douni became sick a long time ago. I still miss Douni and my dad, but instead of being too sad to think about them the coping skills I learned now make me happy to remember them.

Can you think of any challenges that you'd like this book to help you with?

I had a challenge not so long ago. My dad was unwell, and I knew I had sad times ahead. But I'm grateful that my skills helped me cope and move slowly away from the sadness.

I first noticed I had those skills when my dog Douni became sick a long time ago. I still miss Douni and my dad, but instead of being too sad to think about them the coping skills I learned now make me happy to remember them.

This book has lots of great coping skills that will help you with all types of challenges.

A challenge tests our way of coping

We all cope differently. I used to be good at coping with challenges by worrying about them. Did that help? No way!

Then I learned that worry was a waste of brain space because whatever I'd been worried about hadn't happened yet and maybe it never would.

Now I'd rather think of all the ways things could go well.

Reframing challenges

I also used to worry about upcoming school tests. This type of worry can be useful when you learn how to reframe that worry into motivation to prepare for the test.

See? It's all about what you focus on and how you perceive the challenge.

This is what reframing means. You'll learn lots of reframing skills in this book to use when you need help to see challenges differently.

Inner coping skills coach

I'll help you discover your Inner Coping Skills Coach who can cope with absolutely anything. I ask my inner coping skills coach to help me cope with challenges by sprinkling fun onto them. My inner coach makes up all kinds of creative coping skills. You'll get to know how to do that too later in the book.

One of the ways you'll learn is with my 4-step formula to cope with anything.

INTRODUCTION

C. O. P. E. FORMULA	
C = CURIOSITY	Be the CURIOUS detective. Be curious about the challenge.
O = OBSERVER	OBSERVE your thoughts and feelings. Ask: *"What would my inner coping coach say or do instead?"*
P = POSITIVITY	Imagine a POSITIVE outcome. Visualise how you want to solve the challenge, then make up a funny or inspiring affirmation to reframe the challenge.
E = EXPLORER	Think like an EXPLORER! Explore your options. There are lots of new thoughts, feelings and actions you could try as challenges happen. Try taking your inner coping coach's suggested action!

I'll explain how the formula works in the next chapter. How cool will it be when you can cope with anything, anytime just by doing those four steps?

It's important to know you can't stop challenges from popping up, but the difference is you won't be afraid or worried about challenges anymore. You'll know you have what it takes to cope.

Plus, you can help others by sharing your new coping skills. You never know, you might just teach your parents a thing or two about coping with their challenges too. Then if a challenge becomes a little 'tricky', you'll be able to support each other and know what to do.

Imagine saying to your parents someday "Remember your C.O.P.E. skills." Hehe, that would be so much fun!

Coming up next, I will show you how to cope with one of our big challenges, the busy mind monster and you'll learn how to be the boss of your own mind!

Amanda

SLOW YOUR BUSY MIND

The busy mind monster

You wake up, get ready for school, go to school, you play, go to sport, come home, eat, do homework, get ready for bed, and then you're just about to drift off, when….

BOOM!

The busy mind monster chooses to remind you of the entire day! You start to worry about tomorrow! It's on repeat in your mind, it's so hard to stop the mind monster, it feels out of control! UNTIL…

BOOM!

You learn how to be the boss of your mind and switch the monster off.

It's like changing the TV channel or switching the TV off altogether! You become the boss of your mind. In fact, you choose what channel to listen to.

Let's explore lots of fun ways to calm your busy mind and choose the best channels for your mind to focus on.

Your amazing mind

No one else has the exact mind that you have. You're unique. This book helps you look after your mind and keep it focused on things that are helpful to you.

When challenges happen and you think you might not cope, your mind can be the problem or the solution. It can be a mind monster making the problem harder, or it can be the inner coping coach and help you with solutions.

Two little stories

I know a young boy who loves to paint, and he told me he didn't know how to decorate a cake. So, I said "Don't decorate the cake, paint it with colourful icing."

Reframing his creative painting skill changed his ability to believe he could decorate a cake.

A young girl who struggled to speak out loud reframed her challenge when I suggested she write down what she wanted to say. Then I asked her to read out loud what she had written and speaking out aloud became easy.

Organise your mind

If your mind gets messy, consider this strategy to feel in control.

I use imaginary jars with lids. A friend of mine does the same technique with imaginary shoe boxes. A young girl I taught uses imaginary toy boxes and a boy I helped uses pretend tool boxes, like the ones in his dad's garage.

Mind Jars Technique

Step 1: Think of a storage item with a lid (or choose one I've mentioned above).

- I have a jar for school work
- a jar for family stuff
- a jar for worry stuff
- a jar for friends' stuff
- a jar for tomorrow stuff
- jars for past stuff
- a jar for anger stuff
- a general jar for stuff that doesn't fit into other jars

Step 2: If I am having dinner with my family and suddenly my mind is thinking about school work, or worrying about something happening tomorrow, I take a deep breath and imagine my storage jars.

Step 3: I use my mind to pretend opening the lid of the appropriate jar, and I put whatever was worrying me in and close the lid.

Step 4: I continue having dinner (you continue doing what you were doing).

Step 5: After dinner I go to my room. I imagine opening the jar and I use the C.O.P.E. formula to manage the challenge. I allow ten minutes a day to deal with the challenges in the jars.

Be the boss of your mind

Every time an unhelpful thought pops into your head, imagine your inner coping coach is standing beside a rubbish bin and guiding those thoughts into the bin.

Kind of like a good security guard saying "YES, that thought stays, NO, that one goes in the bin."

How to be a good boss?

If you make a decision that makes you happy, but upsets your brother or sister, then take a minute to rethink your decision. Is there a better choice so everyone feels okay?

Mums, dads, brothers, sisters and friends are people too. They have feelings just like you.

> Don't let the angry mind monster be the boss of you.

Would you stick up for your brother or sister if someone was bullying them at school? I imagine most of you would say "yes." Then remember to be kind to them at home too.

If you catch yourself about to be hurtful, ask yourself questions first.
- What will happen if I do?
- What will happen if I don't?

You'll work it out.

Use the exercises in the C.O.P.E. formula below daily, and you'll be able to slow down and train your busy mind.

C.O.P.E. FORMULA FOR A BUSY MIND	
C = CURIOSITY	Be CURIOUS about the thoughts you have. Challenge the ones that are not useful. Sort them into their right containers and let go of the ones that are not helpful or important.
O = OBSERVER	OBSERVE your mind's busy habits, so that you can learn your patterns. Observe how your thoughts make you feel and behave. This helps you get to know yourself better.
P = POSITIVITY	Write a POSITIVE affirmation about what you want instead. E.g. "I feel good about 'A' because I get to choose 'B' instead." Be the boss of your mind by planning when to attend to worries. Don't let your mind be the boss of you.
E = EXPLORER	EXPLORE new ways of being the boss of your busy mind. Make some rules about how you let your thoughts make you feel and behave. Write them down to remind yourself.

Write your affirmation and visualisation ideas here _____

_____

_____

Make a list of all your strengths and describe your happy, peaceful outcome _____

_____

_____

Keep practicing whenever the busy mind monster activates. You have a brain and a mind that can learn new tricks. Being the boss of your mind and using kind thoughts and developing creative ideas for the good of all, means you'll be the best version of yourself you can be.

In Chapter 2, there are lots of skills to help you cope with winning and not winning. You'll learn that both skills are as important as each other.

Remember, don't cop it, COPE with it!

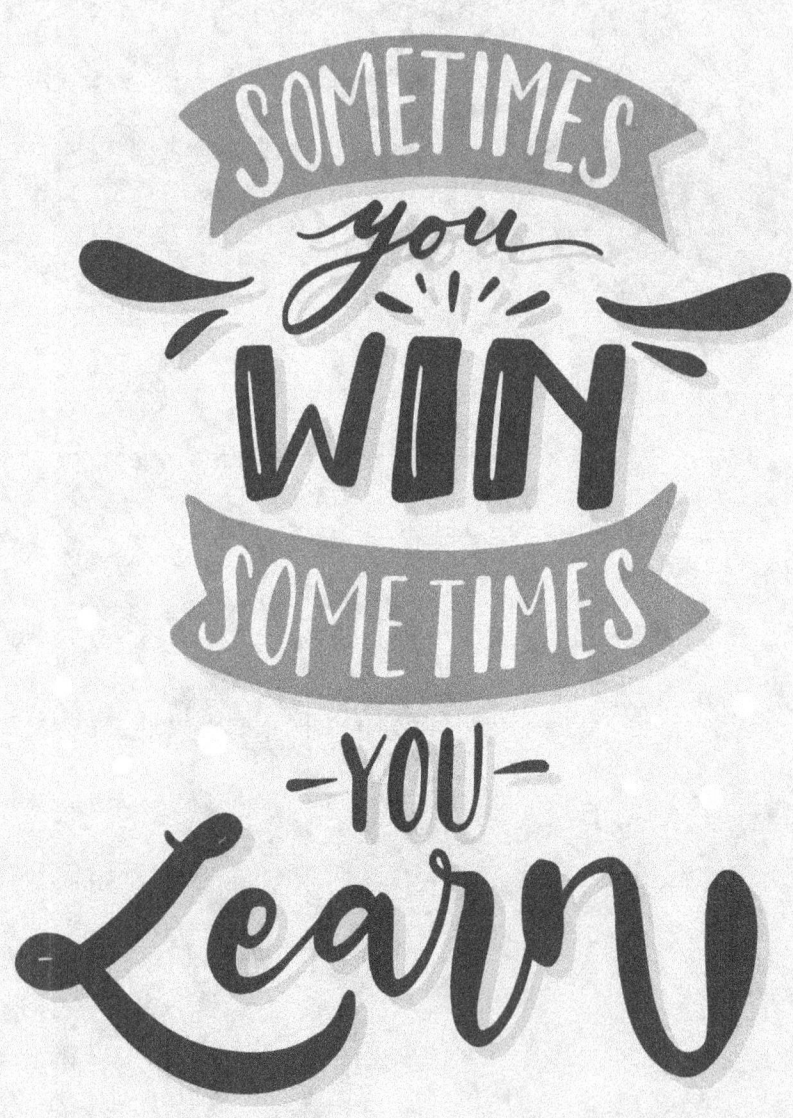

CHAPTER 2

IT'S OKAY TO WIN AND NOT WIN

Have you ever heard someone say, "It's not about winning or losing; it's about how you play the game." Or "Give it a go anyway, it's about being a good sportsperson."

Here's the thing, most successful sports players are the ones who know how to win and how not to win gracefully. They know how to have fun, and to learn and grow, even when they don't win because they've developed a growth mindset.

> **A little story**
>
> A young girl I taught told me that she wouldn't attend her swimming carnival because she knew she wouldn't win. I said, *"Other kids still show up at swimming carnivals or sports days knowing they won't win, and they have fun giving it a go."*
>
> So, what does this young girl need to learn? It's a growth mindset, isn't it!

> When I taught Jamena how to use a growth mindset, she learned to not put as much pressure on herself. She told me, "I have a rule that I made up for myself."
>
> Her rule was "I need to come first."
>
> I explained that this rule had stopped her from learning, growing and having fun with her friends at swimming carnivals.
>
> Jamena changed her rule to a new one that allowed her to have fun and get better at stuff. Her rule was "I choose to give stuff a go."

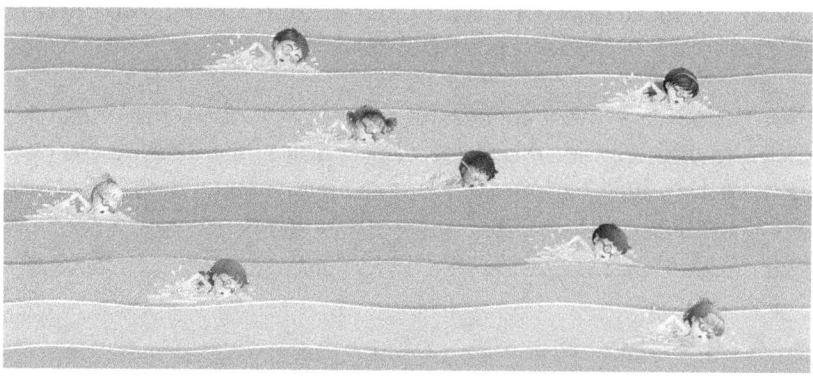

Jamena now looks forward to the carnival because she knows she'll have fun with her friends and enjoy supporting others, while giving it a go herself.

Attitude: what is it?

Attitude is the way you present yourself. What you say and do or how you react.

We're not born with attitudes, we learn them, and the good thing is we can change them.

Attitude activity

Think about your attitude to the things in this list. Is your current attitude helpful or unhelpful? If it's not helpful, think about how you'd prefer to present yourself. I've given you an example to show you what I mean.

TOPIC	CURRENT ATTITUDE	NEW ATTITUDE
Chores	Annoyed and hate doing chores. My parents ask me more than once before I do my chores	I have fun doing my chores first so I can do what I want after I finish
School		
Homework		
Family		
Friends		
Chores		
Dealing with change		
Other		

Your current attitude is based on your beliefs, values and morals. Your parents do a great job teaching you the best that they can. Then you have other influences like what you see on television or the internet, the games you play, and the kids you hang out with. Many things can influence you and contribute to your attitude.

Attitude Hats

Let's pretend an attitude is an invisible hat. You can take a hat off and put it on any time you choose. You can even pick a hat that looks better on you.

Next time you feel unhappy or resentful, or someone is feeling bad about something you said or did, think about the attitude hat you were wearing. Can you take that hat off and choose a different hat?

Did that hat say 'Mr. or Miss Calm?' Or was it the drama hat? Was it the team player or jealous friend hat?

Think about school or your interactions with friends. What attitude hats do you wear? After school, what attitude hat do you come home with?

Sometimes we have worn an Attitude Hat so often we are given a label of being the person who is always this or that; happy, sad, respectful, disrespectful.

If the label on your Attitude Hat is not a nice one, it's lucky you can change it. Having the right attitude can help you be successful. Not just with learning, but with how you win and not win. Attitude is your outfit so pick a good one.

> Sometimes we have worn an Attitude Hat so often we are given a label of being the person who is always this or that; happy, sad, respectful, disrespectful.

How to improve your attitude to winning and not winning

Whether it is sports, academic competition or competition against yourself to compete for a personal best, what matters is how you behave about the outcome. You'll be remembered for the attitude you showed when you won, and when you didn't.

Think about how you cope when someone performs better than you. The best type of competition attitude is when you can honestly say you prepared enough, no matter the outcome. Have the attitude to accept that you either did the best that you could or accept the truth that you could have prepared better.

> The best type of competition attitude is when you can honestly say you prepared enough, no matter the outcome.

Choose to be curious about attitudes you've had that have held you back and design your new attitude to be game ready for both winning and not winning.

Honest assessment

Assess what you learned about yourself, the competition and other competitors. When we have a flexible attitude to winning and not winning, we are less likely to give up. Then we can learn from winning or not winning, prepare and give it another go.

Your best is always good enough. You don't need to live up to impossible or unrealistic expectations. It's good to make others proud, but the most important person in the equation is you.

The winning journey

Winning isn't always about coming first. Sometimes you know you can't win. It's important to look at your expectations and how you play the game. Look at how you supported others and helped them go the distance too. You might not score a goal, but you'll be acknowledged for team-play when you set up a goal or defend well and stop the opposing team's goal.

Winning is also about a sense of achievement in how you handled whatever happened. It doesn't have to be about a game. You can feel a sense of winning achievement when you finish a book or complete a great drawing or do a great job cleaning your room.

> You can feel a sense of winning achievement when you finish a book or complete a great drawing or do a great job cleaning your room.

What happens if you don't win?

Have you ever met anyone who always wins at everything?
The truth is if you don't win every time, it means you're human.

Not winning also gives you the opportunity to be happy for someone else who did. In fact, that's an important experience to feel.

C.O.P.E. FORMULA FOR WINNING AND NOT WINNING	
C = CURIOSITY	Become CURIOUS about the attitude hats you wear at different times. Notice how you or others describe you e.g., sore loser, or good sportsperson.
O = OBSERVER	Become an expert OBSERVER and commentator who can see from every angle. What attitude hat have you been wearing when you like or don't like things? What would your inner coping coach recommend?
P = POSITIVITY	Imagine a competitive POSITIVE scenario. Visualise the way you are remembered for having a great attitude to both winning and not winning. Repeat positive affirmations like "I always do my best."
E = EXPLORER	EXPLORE ways to be happy for yourself and other kids whether it's a win, lose or neutral situation. What words and actions can you use?

Write your affirmation or visualisation ideas here _____

_____

_____

_____

What is your new rule for winning or not winning? _____

_____

_____

_____

Whenever you recognise an attitude hat that stops you from being your best version, pause, do the C.O.P.E. formula, and try out a new hat!

Let's move on to Chapter 3 where I help you develop skills to cope with unkind thoughts and words.

Remember, don't cop it, COPE with it!

CHAPTER 3

DEALING WITH UNKIND THOUGHTS AND WORDS

A little story

When Frances was a kid at school, she remembers doing a test in maths and some kids were talking and made it difficult to concentrate. She asked them nicely to stop and went back to her test.

The girl sitting next to her began saying unkind things about her. She replied politely that the noise was distracting her, but she was told she was selfish.

She remembers feeling hurt and confused. She wanted to do well on the test, but felt the hot tears burning her eyes. She kept quiet and didn't say anything back.

Later she told her mother about it and shared how she felt. Talking about it made her feel much better.

Unkind thoughts and words

Unkind words can be deliberate or unintentional, but once they are heard they can sometimes plant a seed of self-doubt. Our mind is like a sponge and it can feed on unkind thoughts and words. Those thoughts sprout in the brain like branches of trees. If we don't know how to stop them, those branches can affect our confidence.

These words and thoughts can be said to you by other people, but nasty words and thoughts can also be said or thought by us about others and ourselves.

It is important to realise that when you become aware of unkindness, you can take charge of your reaction and switch it off. Become a curious detective on thought patrol!

> Become a curious detective on thought patrol!

What to do when unkind things are said to you

If someone says something unkind to you, or you have unkind thoughts, simply decide how long you want to hold on to the thoughts before you let them go. This means you set your own rules.

If the unkindness hurt, it's important to give it a small fraction of attention at first so that you can resolve the hurt. Become the curious detective and consider what it was about the words or thoughts that hurt.

It's not about blaming yourself or others for the words, it's so you can learn why you were triggered to feel that way.

Letting unkindness go

Step 1: Be grateful for the opportunity to let it go.
Step 2: Decide the only opinion that matters is yours. Other people's opinions are not important.
Step 3: Acknowledge the sensation of hurt and breathe fresh air into the place in the body or head where you felt the hurt. (You might need to take 3 or 4 breaths to do this fully).
Step 4: Say to yourself, *"I approve of myself."*

This is a great skill to practice.

Another fun way to let hurt go

Imagine unkind thoughts and words are like a bird who poops on you, or a fly who lands on your food. Imagine you can wash the poopy words off or simply shoo them away like a fly.

DEALING WITH UNKIND THOUGHTS AND WORDS

Moving past unkind thoughts and words

Occasionally there will be some thoughts that seem to get stuck repeating themselves in your mind. If this happens to me, I reach out to a friend.

Some kids keep inspirational cards in their school bag, lunch box or pencil case. They read a card when they want to focus on something positive instead. This way they take control of the space in their head. For example, a boy called Jack carries an inspiring quote inside his pencil case that says, *"Be brave Jack, speak up."* Jack designed the quote himself and used his favourite happy colours too.

Stop holding on

Words are just words and thoughts are just thoughts. They only affect you if you give them power by holding onto them.

If you're the one responsible for unkind thoughts and words, simply choose to stop saying or thinking them. Start practicing more kindness.

You can always ask an adult who speaks kind words for advice. You may or may not agree, but you always learn by listening to others. You get to decide what suits you best.

The forgiveness 'whatever' mind-bin

Call upon your inner coping skills coach to throw unkind words into the *"whatever"* mind-bin. If you don't have this mind-bin, create one right now.

Fun activity:

Close your eyes and take a minute to imagine your version of a *whatever* mind-bin,' store it somewhere in your head.

Take a minute to think of something unkind someone has said or done to you. Pick up the unkindness, you could scrunch it up, or rip it to shreds and screw it into a ball, then dump that unkindness into the 'whatever mind-bin.'

Turn the corners of your mouth into a smile and say with lots of fun energy, "*Whatever!*"

If you catch yourself being mean to yourself, dump it in the *whatever* mind-bin' too!

Then:

- Look for evidence of everything that is right about you.

We often remind ourselves of what's wrong with us, but do you remind yourself of what's right? Look for more of that evidence, there's plenty to find.

\multicolumn{2}{c}{**C.O.P.E. FORMULA FOR DEALING WITH UNKIND THOUGHTS AND WORDS**}
C = CURIOSITY	Become the CURIOUS detective and challenge unkindness with your powerful mind. Create a '*whatever* mind-bin'
O = OBSERVER	OBSERVE how unkindness makes you feel. Use your "*whatever* mind bin" to throw away the unkindness. Use your inner coping coach to let it go and choose how you want to feel instead.
P = POSITIVITY	Replace unkindness by smiling POSITIVELY and straighten your posture. Write down 3 or 4 positive things about yourself in the space below. Never accept unkindness as the truth anymore. Negativity doesn't belong in your head or body.
E = EXPLORER	EXPLORE new ways to respond to unkindness. Keep practicing getting good at letting unkindness go.

Write positive affirmations about being kind and speaking kind words _____

_____

_____

_____

Make a list of the good things about yourself. Practice positive visualisations remembering those good things_____

_____

_____

_____

_____

Remember, practice makes you a better person. Whether it's coping skills or a sport or studying for a test. You get better the more you practice.

In the following chapter I have more coping skills to help you manage pressure and stressful times. Let's do this!

Don't cop it! C.O.P.E. with it!

CHAPTER 4

MANAGING PRESSURE AND UNHELPFUL STRESS

Some people might think that pressure and stress are the same. But pressure is external and is normally out of your control, while stress is the result when you don't have coping skills to handle whatever pressure is happening.

> You can't often control the pressure.
> But you can always control the stress you feel about the pressure
> (once you know how.)

You can't often control the pressure.
But you can always control the stress you feel about the pressure (once you know how.)

External pressure vs internal stress

What do I mean by external pressure?

Pressure lives 'outside' of you, but you decide whether to make it internal by bringing it inside your body or head as stress.

Think of the pressure of school or in the case of adults, the pressure of work.

School and work are external things, thank goodness! If you leave that pressure where it belongs, on the outside, you can control your stress by planning around the pressure.

Consider the pressure of homework due tomorrow. You can't control the pressure of getting homework, but you can control how you handle it.

You can do the homework as soon as you get home then have the rest of the night off. Or you can leave it to build up as stressful pressure by doing it at the last minute before class.

> School and work are external things, thank goodness! If you leave that pressure where it belongs, on the outside, you can control your stress by planning around the pressure.

Let the pressure exist but choose not to create more. Be clear on your responsibilities. If you have a homework task, just do your task. The task is usually far less stressful than you build it up to be in your mind. If the task is a little harder or longer than you hoped, break it up into smaller tasks that you can handle easily.

A little story

I asked a year 3 student to complete a mindset questionnaire so I could learn how to help him better in our tutoring sessions.

For example, he was struggling with 'growth mindset'. When he made errors in maths questions, he became embarrassed but wouldn't ask his teachers for help. His embarrassment meant he was missing out on learning.

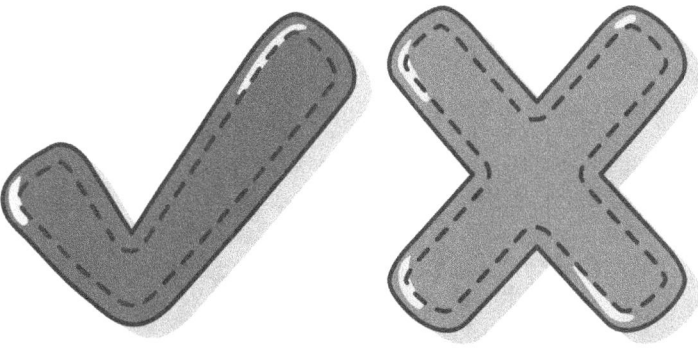

I taught him the C.O.P.E. skills and, with tutoring, in his next questionnaire his results showed he now accepted it was okay to make mistakes. He no longer felt ashamed of errors and realised that errors were a useful tool to show him what he needed to learn.

All it took to 'take the pressure off' was an attitude shift. To take off the 'fear of making mistakes attitude hat' and replace it with a better one.

What role does your imagination play?

Your imagination can often create disasters out of minor pressures.

Let's say your bus is late and you begin to worry you'll miss your first class. You might start to imagine crazy reasons why the bus could be late.

Your mind starts with heavy traffic, and escalates quickly to a horrible crash, or you fret that you won't get to school for hours and you'll miss the test and fail the class. Meanwhile, the bus is only 5 minutes late and you may still get to school on time.

What would happen if you changed the way you told your story?

If you changed the way you told your story, you'd feel much less pressure. Sometimes we create a story that feels like we're carrying a whole bunch of bricks in our bag. But if we change our story to be a short and factual one, we get the opportunity to throw away some bricks and feel much lighter.

> If you changed the way you told your story, you'd feel much less pressure.

Imagine you have a test coming up

- Do you create lots of drama about the test?
- Tell everyone, even the bus driver, you'll probably fail?
- Do you build it up to be a bigger deal than it needs to be, then carry around lots of stress about it?

Imagine what would change if you shortened the story to something like *"I have a test so I plan to study like this… (make a plan). When I plan, I can still enjoy my usual stuff."*

It can be that simple. It's all in your attitude to the story and the planning to manage it.

> It can be that simple. It's all in your attitude to the story and the planning to manage it.

Create your rules

Write out your rules to help you deal with pressure.

The facts are: you have no control over external pressures (e.g. the bus is late, or the homework or test you have been given).

But you do have control over the internal stress you choose to create about it.

Play with writing your rules. Here are some suggestions you might consider:

Rule 1: I always make a plan to handle what is asked of me
Rule 2: I always base my story on facts
Rule 3: I let imagined dramas fade
Rule 4: I'm in charge of the pressures I create for myself
Rule 5: Other people's pressures belong to them, not me

Other people's pressure and stress

Sometimes, as a good friend, you might want to help people through tough times. That's wonderful, but it's important not to use their pressures as an excuse to procrastinate on yours. Or to pretend that their drama story and stress is yours too. Be compassionate, supportive and generous. But own what is yours and let go of the rest.

What is your responsibility and what isn't?

This is an easy one. If it's out of your control then it's not your responsibility, but it doesn't mean that you don't behave responsibly. You just need to know what's in your control and what's not.

You can ask an adult to help you work out if pressures are in your control or not.

Ask your inner coping coach. Challenge your imagination and if it's getting carried away with the drama, be the boss of your mind by reminding yourself of the facts.

Other kids' reactions are not yours

Just because other kids are reacting to external pressure or feeling stressed about their drama story it doesn't mean you need to.

If you can help them without falling into their pressure, then do so.

C.O.P.E. FORMULA FOR MANAGING PRESSURE AND STRESS	
C = CURIOSITY	Become the CURIOUS detective and challenge the internal stress you place on yourself. Notice the difference between external pressure and internal stress.
O = OBSERVER	OBSERVE your reactions and be the boss of your mind. Would your inner coping coach ask you to change the way you speak about things?
P = POSITIVITY	In the space below, make a list of the POSITIVE things you can control. Use an affirmation to help you focus on the positive outcome.
E = EXPLORER	EXPLORE what you need to do to stay out of the chaos and drama. Think about your current pressures and make a plan or ask for help.

Make a list of the practical things you can do to manage pressure and stress _____

_____

_____

_____

Write out your rules and your positive visualisation remembering you are in control _____

_____

_____

_____

Remember, pressures are external. You can't control if your teacher gives you a test, but you can control how you prepare for it to reduce your stress levels.

In the next chapter we'll look at the challenge of worry. Let's learn the easy way to switch worry off and move away from it.

Don't cop it! C.O.P.E. with it!

CHAPTER 5

DEALING WITH WORRY

A little story

There was a young boy who was very worried about going to the dentist.

A trusted adult said, "*Sometimes the worry is like one big bubble with lots of little bubbles inside. Some of the little bubbles include lots of smaller worries that we make out to be worse in our mind than they really are.*"

The adult showed the little boy how to close his eyes and look at every little bubble and say hello to them all. When the boy did this, most of the bubbles popped immediately. For those that were left, the adult told the boy to pop them himself with an imaginary pin.

The boy laughed at how easy it was to pop the bubbles and realised he immediately felt less worried.

When the boy looked back at the big bubble it was a lot smaller.

The adult told him to look at the big bubble and say, *"Thank you for trying to protect me, I don't need you anymore."*

The boy laughed again as the big bubble of worry popped too.

The Worrier

To determine if something is worth worrying about ask, *"Is there something I can do about it right now?"*

I remember I was worried about a decision I had to make. I did not need to make that decision for 2 days.

While I was worrying, I was not paying attention.
- I missed learning a key topic in mathematics class
- I was distracted by worry and made mistakes playing netball
- The worry caused me stress and I had conflict at home

When I look back now, I wish I'd asked myself if there was something I could do about the decision at that time.

The answer was; there was nothing I could do *just yet*.

I only needed to allocate five or ten minutes to think about my decision at the appropriate time when I could do something about the outcome. Instead I had spent days worrying and letting that worry mess with other stuff.

Imagine this scenario

Pretend it's Saturday and you have music practice in an hour, but you forgot your instrument. It's still in your locker at school. That makes you worry about whether or not you locked your locker.

"Oh no," you think. *"What if someone steals my instrument?"*

Your creative imagination starts to have a party with the worry. It escalates and you spend the weekend stressing, biting your fingernails and scared to tell your parents in case the instrument gets stolen.

Can you do something about finding your musical instrument right now? Let's assume you can't get access to the school to check, so the answer is a big fat NO!

Coping skill – make a plan:

1. Schedule to get up 15 minutes earlier to get the early bus to school on Monday, or tell your parent and ask them to

drive you to school earlier (now that's two worries you can switch off, you're not hiding it from your parents either)
2. Plan to go straight to your locker and check before you do anything else
3. Now you are free from worrying about it all weekend

> The truth is, worry won't change anything except your level of suffering

The truth is, worry won't change anything except your level of suffering

Visualise releasing worries

- Place your worry on a cloud and let it float away
- Load your worry onto a freight train and let the train disappear
- Place your worries into a rocket ship and send it through the solar system, landing on different planets and dropping off worries along the way

DEALING WITH WORRY

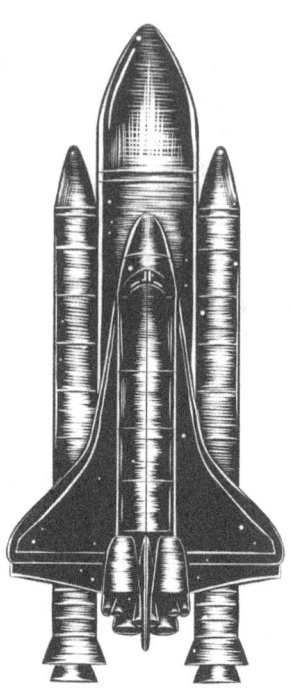

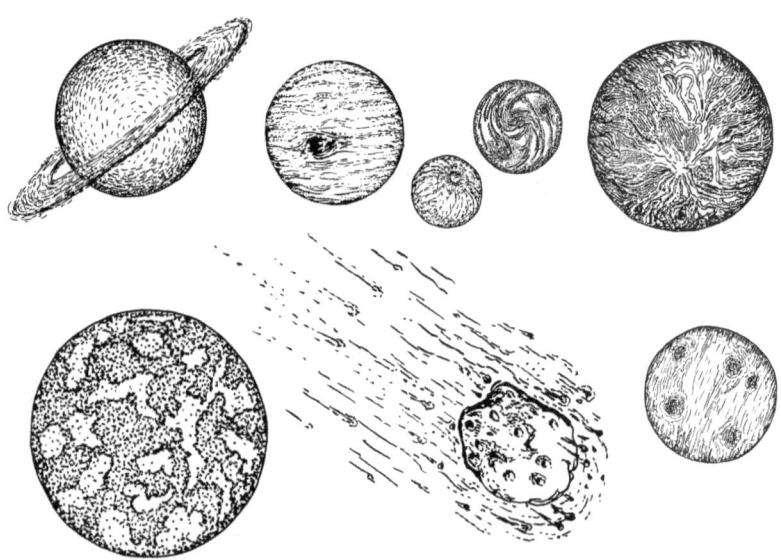

Take action to eliminate real worries

If you can do something about the worry right now, then:
1. Plan the action you need to take and
2. Take the action

It really could be that simple

Open your mindset to a new way of thinking about the worry. Perhaps it's not as big as your imagination created it to be.

> Plan the action you need to take. Worries don't need to totally disappear, but you can have more control over them.

Plan the action you need to take. Worries don't need to totally disappear, but you can have more control over them.

C.O.P.E. FORMULA FOR DEALING WITH WORRY	
C = CURIOSITY	Become the CURIOUS detective and challenge the worry. Sort the worries into those that you can do something about now, those you can't do anything about yet and those that don't really matter.
O = OBSERVER	OBSERVE whether your imagination is getting carried away with the images and stories that it creates.
P = POSITIVITY	Write out your POSITIVE plan of action (ask an adult or your inner coping coach for help). Visualise letting it go using one of the chapter examples or your own.
E = EXPLORER	EXPLORE the possibility of whether your mind is holding onto the worry for a reason? Can you simply say 'no' to it and put it in the *'whatever'* mind-bin? And then get on with what you were doing?

Make a list of the practical things you can do to deal with worry

_____

_____

_____

Write out your positive visualisation to let worry go or your plan to deal with the worry _____

_____

_____

Remember, you can only control the worry that you can take action about right this minute. If you can't do anything about it right now, make a plan for when you can. Then park the worry till you can solve it and get on with life.

In the next chapter there are lots of coping skills to move away from anger. Don't forget to start practicing the coping skills you already have so far.

Don't cop it! C.O.P.E. with it!

CHAPTER 6

LETTING GO OF ANGER

A little story

There was a child who was always angry at things and people.

"He makes me angry…she makes me angry…this makes me angry…and that too."

He even began to notice how often he felt angry, but he didn't know what to do about it.

I listened as he told me that everything around him could make him angry.

He was basically saying his anger was not his fault. That everyone and everything else 'made' him angry. *"It's not my fault, they make me angry,"* he said. Right?

The boy couldn't have been more wrong, he just didn't know it yet.

Imagine this scenario:

You unintentionally break my favourite cup.

I can either choose to be angry or I can be sad, or disappointed, or some other reaction.

Or, I could choose to help you not feel so bad about breaking it. You probably already feel bad; I don't need to add to your distress about the cup.

So, let's go back to this boy. He found it easier to access anger and let his behaviour follow his angry mood.

In the scenario of the broken cup, he possibly would have been angry at me and said, *"It's your fault for giving me your favourite cup."*

It eventually got to the stage where the boy realised he couldn't control the anger anymore.

You see, we get good at what we practice. And if you practice anger, then you get good at it. Until you decide to let the pattern of anger go.

The boy decided to work on his 'inner self.' He called it his 'inner wizard.' He learned to acknowledge his angry feelings; they were his, no-one else could 'make' him angry. He had chosen in the past to react with anger.

He learned to assess if the anger was an acceptable reaction and to choose different responses. This generally made him much happier and he became good at letting the anger go safely without blaming everyone and everything.

But it took practice.

> You see, we get good at what we practice. And if you practice anger, then you get good at it. Until you decide to let the pattern of anger go.

Is anger a normal emotion?

Anger is a normal emotion, so it's important not to ignore it.

The trick is to accept that feelings of anger happen. Just like happiness is an emotion that makes you feel a certain way; anger is also an emotion with energy that triggers different feelings and sensations.

Even though I've said that anger is normal, it's the way you handle and act out the anger that makes it abnormal and potentially hurtful to you and others.

Even though anger is normal it's what you do with it that counts

Do you have a brother or sister or a friend that sometimes makes you angry?

NO! The correct answer is no-one can 'make' you angry. YOU decided that what they did annoyed you, and then you let yourself become angry.

> **Let's test this**
>
> **Scenario one:** Your brother or sister plays with one of your things. "Noooo," I hear you yell from the other side of the street. You freak out in anger at your brother or sister!
>
> **Scenario two:** Your friend comes to visit and plays with your things without asking. You are totally chilled about it.

GOTCHA. You choose to react angrily or not, depending on who plays with your 'things'. You choose how you respond.

Is it bad to be angry?

It's not bad to be angry, but it's not okay to take your anger out on others. You need boundaries.

> It's not bad to be angry, but it's not okay to take your anger out on others. You need boundaries.

Boundaries are like rules to keep you on track. A sports field has boundaries that help control the game. We also need boundaries inside us such as anger boundaries. These link to our moral boundaries like respect and speaking kindly to others. Think about your anger boundaries. What have they looked like so far? If the boundaries need to change, what should they be?

What makes you angry?

Think about what makes you angry, it's different for everybody. Is it when you feel hurt by people's words or actions?

It's important to be aware of your personal triggers for anger so you can learn how to manage those situations without adding more hurt or anger.

You may need to recognise that it's only you that allows the anger to grow. Anger is only meant to be a short term burst of energy to tell you it's time to deal with something differently.

What is anger trying to tell you?

Maybe you've been treated unfairly, and you have a right to feel angry. Anger is telling you something isn't right, but your logical mind doesn't work when you're angry, so the decisions you make when you're angry are usually ones you regret later.

Have you ever said something in anger and lashed out only later to feel guilty about how badly you acted? That's because your emotional mind can't think logically yet.

Anger tells you something is not right. Be grateful for this message, notice it and then decide what to do next, once you are no longer angry. Remember, to learn coping skills we need to develop a 'growth mindset' and this is an opportunity to expand that mindset.

A great way is to ask yourself questions and listen to your answers. Ponder the answers and the anger will cool.

Anger is a message that something needs to be said or done

When you are triggered to feel anger, try the following steps:

1. Pause
2. Ask "Why am I feeling angry?"
3. Listen to the message that your body and mind is giving you
4. Thank the anger for bringing it to your attention
5. Breathe the anger out or put it on a cloud and watch it go, load it into your space rocket and send it to the moon
6. Then take calm action on the situation that triggered the anger

Anger only becomes a problem when you don't listen to it, or when the anger is handled inappropriately.

Anger is just a form of energy

If you need to convert that angry energy into physical movements try doing five push-ups, or star jumps or whatever exercise you like.

Other ways to use the energy of anger safely

- Shake your body fast, shake it out, let the energy drain out of your fingertips as you shake.
- Wash your hands clean of anger, if you can't physically wash them, imagine it.
- Self-talk is also helpful when you feel angry.

> **Why letting go of anger is helpful**
>
> When you let go of anger you have less stress. It helps reduce anxiety and worry and makes you a nicer person to be around.
>
> It's also better for your physical body too. When you're angry your body is tense, you won't be able to play sports and be your best if you're all tense and stressed.
>
> If you let go of anger you'll think clearer and have a better memory so your school results will be better too.

Other ways to let anger go?

Here are a few ways to let go of anger, choose what fits best for you or make up another way. Anger is invisible so you can do anything you like with it.

- You can blow it into a balloon and set it free
- You can write it out onto paper and tear it up and throw it in the bin
- Try washing it away in the shower
- Put the anger into a burp or a pop off and let it out if you like, ha-ha!
- Imagine the anger leaving your body as a colour through your feet into the earth

Just remember to let it go…

\	C.O.P.E. FORMULA FOR LETTING GO OF ANGER
C = CURIOSITY	Become the CURIOUS detective and challenge the angry reaction. Look for other ways to respond, as suggested in the chapter.
O = OBSERVER	OBSERVE what makes you angry and what it does to your body. You are in control of how you think and how you react. What would your inner coping coach advise?
P = POSITIVITY	Write out your POSITIVE plan to let go of anger. Use a positive affirmation *"I have permission to let go of anger."* And then visualise letting it go.
E = EXPLORER	EXPLORE how you react to other people when they're angry. Also explore how people who are calm control themselves and stay calm. Look for opportunities to practice a better version of yourself.

Make a list of the things that make you angry and what anger is trying to tell you _____

_____

_____

Create an affirmation and write a positive visualisation of how you can let anger go. What would you do to release the angry energy?

_____

_____

_____

Remember, you get to choose whether you react with anger or curiosity. You get to give yourself a chance to release the anger without spilling that anger onto other people.

In the next chapter I've provided lots of coping skills to move away from sadness. This is an emotion that happens to all of us at some point. So, learning how to cope with sadness now will make it easier next time you're sad.

Don't cop it! C.O.P.E. with it!

AMANDA DOUNIS

Everything Will Be Ok

CHAPTER 7

MOVING AWAY FROM SADNESS

The importance of time

When it comes to sadness and all the things that make us sad people, often say, *"Time heals."*

You might think to yourself *"How much time will it take?"*

Well the truth is, it depends on two things… you and what the sadness is. *(If you lose a pet, your sadness may last longer than if you lose your favourite skates.)*

So, instead of trying to find out how long it will take till you feel better, how about you accept that you'll heal in your own time and at your own pace. Feeling sad is an important part of the process. We can learn ways to cope with sadness and gradually move away from it when the time is right.

If you look way back in your life at times when you were sad, you don't feel as sad about most of those times right now do you? Some things you may have even forgotten about.

So, it's true, time does heal, but there are ways you can learn how to cope with sadness when it happens.

I don't think it's healthy to keep our head and memories full of sad stuff, there'd be no room for the good memories!

How long does it take?

You might be a person that takes a little longer, or someone who moves away from sadness quickly, accepts it and learns from it. That's great as long as you're not hiding the sadness and pretending it's not there.

Will it always feel like this?

Your sadness will not feel the same forever. Each time that you feel sad about something, it'll be a different type of sadness.

Let's do this exercise

Think of a time in the past when you felt sad about something.

Compare what it felt like when it first happened and how you feel today.

What you feel now will be different. This means you processed it and you feel less emotional pain about it now.

Think back to my introduction when my dog Douni and my dad passed away. When I think of them now, it's a different feeling than when it first happened. I miss them now, but I can feel happy and remember how much I loved them without feeling the pain of sadness I felt when it first happened.

That's called processing the sadness and coping with it.

Getting stuck in sadness

Feeling sad is normal, but if you feel stuck on a sad emotion for a long time, it's best to chat with a trusted adult like a parent, teacher, school counsellor, relative, or someone you think is right for you.

What if I don't know why I'm sad?

If you feel sad but nothing obvious has happened to make you feel that way, it's important to tell someone too.

Sometimes a friend or family member may notice this before you think you're ready to talk about it. You're being noticed, not judged, and it means they care about you and want to help. Sometimes we all need a little help to deal with our feelings.

Sadness is often triggered by change you didn't want or expect

- Like if you are told your family has to move to a new house or move schools so you have to leave behind some great stuff like friends and that feeling of comfort at school, or your old bedroom.
- When someone says something to hurt you or ignore you.
- Family or friendship upsets.
- We can be sad when we lose a game or break or misplace something valuable.

Change doesn't always have to trigger sadness

You may choose to feel excited about change, but for the purpose of learning coping skills let's pretend for a minute that you're feeling sad because you have to move to a new house and go to a new school.

Imagine, what it would feel like if you were excited to explore your new home and set up your new bedroom. The amazing slumber parties you can have when your old friends come to visit or when you visit them.

You get to choose which Attitude Hat you wear about change. The one that feels sad and resentful because you have to move, or the one that feels excited and anticipates the adventure.

Soothing rituals

There are helpful things you can do to move away from sadness. You can do activities or rituals to help soothe yourself.

Have you ever needed to comfort yourself by holding your favourite teddy or blanket when you were younger? Or spend time with someone like a parent, or even a pet, just to feel their warmth?

After my dog Douni died I developed a soothing ritual that I still do. I stroke his photo every now and then and leave him a doggy biscuit. It's really helped me move away from sadness in my own special way.

Life and daily activities still continue even when you're sad

To avoid being stuck in sadness it's important to do your best to be part of daily activities, even while you're processing sadness.

Imagine the local library or supermarket, or your school. I bet there are plenty of people who still turn up for work despite personal sadness. Sometimes it's about the distraction of interacting with familiar activities that helps give the mind time to process and heal.

It's important however that you don't use distractions to avoid the sadness altogether. That's just another way that will keep you stuck. It's finding the right balance of being busy, and also self-care.

If you're unsure, reach out to a trusted adult who knows how to self-care and handle sadness well.

Respecting emotions like sadness

Remember in the chapter on letting go of anger, I mentioned you need to listen to what the anger has to say in order to help you change it. Well, it's the same with sadness (and other emotions too).

Every emotion we have has a message for us, emotions are feedback on our world and how we are coping with it.

Your emotions are normal, they are part of you, look after yourself by listening to them.

> Every emotion we have has a message for us, emotions are feedback on our world and how we are coping with it.

Activity

Every now and then check in with your emotions and ask, "*How am I coping today?*" Listen respectfully and call upon your inner coping coach to ask how you can support yourself or self-soothe.

> Emotions are part of us, so we need to care for them. Not just the sad ones but also the angry, frustrated and happy ones. There's always a reason why emotions show up.

Instead of being scared of or confused by emotions, choose any of the C.O.P.E. strategies in the book to help address the emotions as they come up.

C.O.P.E. FORMULA FOR MOVING AWAY FROM SADNESS	
C = CURIOSITY	Become the CURIOUS detective and be compassionate toward yourself. Ask *"How is this sadness affecting me?"*
O = OBSERVER	OBSERVE what makes you sad. Choose a growth mindset by listening to what your sadness is teaching you.
P = POSITIVITY	Write out your POSITIVE plan to create a soothing ritual that will honour your sadness. Create an affirmation "I have permission to move away from this sadness as time passes."
E = EXPLORER	EXPLORE other emotions that you may need to process. Perhaps journal weekly about how you are feeling until you process the sadness.

Make a list of the things that you can do to deal with and move away from sadness _____

_____

_____

Write a positive visualisation about a ritual that may help you process sadness _____

_____

_____

Remember, you get to choose whether you see your emotions as helpful or unhelpful. Sadness can be a gift of wisdom too. And remember to ask a trusted adult for help if you suspect you have been stuck in sadness (or other emotions) for too long, especially if they are taking the joy away from other parts of your life.

In the next chapter we'll talk about making the most of your relationships. These could be relationships with your family, friends or your gadgets!

Remember, don't cop it! C.O.P.E. with it!

CHAPTER 8

MAKING THE MOST OF RELATIONSHIPS

Have you ever said, *"It's not my fault,"* when it was?

Have you ever got in trouble for something you didn't do because someone else said, *"It's not my fault,"* and it was?

Feels yuck on both sides doesn't it? One side leaves you feeling guilty if someone else gets into trouble for what you did. The other means you feel unfairly treated because you didn't do what you're accused of.

> **A little story**
>
> I remember helping a young girl called Katie who felt guilty because her big sister got into trouble for something Katie had done.
>
> *"Who broke the good china vase that grandma gave me?"* asked mum.

> Katie glanced at her sister and said with certainty, *"Not me!"*
>
> Katie's sister insisted she hadn't done it either. Mom was upset that no-one was telling the truth and punished both of them.
>
> Katie and her sister were grounded, and the worst thing was her sister knew that Katie was guilty.
>
> Months later Katie still felt so guilty. She'd hadn't talked to her sister about it and it felt like they'd grown further apart. She thought her sister must hate her.

What do you think was happening?

Was Katie's guilt making her see her relationship with her sister differently? Had what Katie done now interfered with the way she communicated with her sister?

I told Katie that the only way she would ever know what her sister was thinking was to talk to her about it.

Katie agreed. After they talked, Katie realised it was her own guilt over her dishonesty that had come between her and her sister.

"Why didn't you tell on me?" She asked her sister.

"By then it didn't matter," her sister said. *"I knew I was innocent and that's all that mattered."*

Katie's sister had processed her anger and let it go. It was Katie who had held onto the guilt which meant she had felt uncomfortable in her relationship with her sister.

After asking a group of kids who rated their relationships with their family and friends as 10 out of 10, the top four things that stood out for everyone I asked were:

1. They have the ability to let go of stuff that comes up in their relationships
2. They don't let things bother them for too long
3. They don't take things too personally
4. They talked things through and forgave because the relationship was important to them

The different types of relationships

The most common relationships we think of are the ones with other people; family, friends, the community and yes, in a few years, even the person you like 'that way'! But we also have relationships with animals, and even our phones, and other things we have developed attachments to, like our clothes, special things in our bedroom, and our gadgets.

Relationship is simply your connection and attachment to someone or something. Sometimes those connections are smooth and sometimes they can get a little rocky.

> Sometimes those connections are smooth and sometimes they can get a little rocky.

Activity

Take a moment and think about a time you couldn't find something special to you, or when something you treasured stopped working, or got ruined.

Remember Katie's story from the beginning of the chapter? Let's think about this a little more because there are layers to the relationships we see in that story:

1. Katie's mother had a relationship with the vase that Grandma had given her. Often the relationship is not about the 'thing', it's actually about the meaning attached to it. In this case, it was the connection with Grandma that Katie's mother valued in the vase.
2. Katie's sister had a relationship of trust with her. When Katie broke that trust, her sister, although angry at first, recognised Katie's fear and valued her relationship to her sister more than the anger. She let the anger go and forgave Katie.
3. Katie's relationship to two things mattered more than her fear of telling the truth. Her relationship with honesty felt out of alignment and she missed her relationship with her sister. The need to smooth the relationships again over-ruled her fear of being found out.

As you can see, there are many layers to relationships which is why sometimes they can get a little rocky.

Relationship balance - what happens when one relationship affects another?

Sometimes one relationship begins to take up more of our time and this affects how you handle other relationships, sometimes not in a good way.

For example, if your relationship with screen time has started to take over, then there's less time to spend on relationships with friends, homework, pets, family or outdoor activities.

Think about your relationships – are they in balance?

Make a list of all the human, pet, inanimate objects and gadget relationships you have. Are they in balance? Are you spending too much time on any one relationship? Is there one that distracts you from another important relationship affecting them in a negative way?

If so, ask yourself:

- *"What can I do to rebalance?"*
- *"Am I willing to do that?"*

The importance of relationships

The most important thing about relationships is they help us feel connected, supported and create a sense of belonging. When a relationship feels positive everything else tends to feel good too.

For example, kids that have good relationships with their teachers enjoy the class and often get better results too.

Your relationship with yourself

Let's focus on the relationship you have with yourself.

How do you speak to yourself?

- With kindness or judgement?
- Encouragement or accusation?
- Do you believe in yourself or doubt yourself?
- Do you compare yourself to others to make yourself feel bad?

Remember in the first few chapters, I asked you to call upon your inner coping coach? Your coping coach can help you practice how you speak to yourself and have the best relationship of all.

If you don't like you, you'll never believe that others do, no matter how much they say they do.

Use self-talk to forgive yourself when you make a mistake and ask your inner coping coach, *"What can I learn from this?"*

> If you don't like you, you'll never believe that others do, no matter how much they say they do.

Mistakes are how we learn and grow

Mistakes are your chance for growth, for feedback on how you're going. Mistakes inside relationships are an opportunity for honesty and learning. One thing you need is the courage to keep communicating, even when things feel tough.

Things you can do to keep communication open

When communication stops in relationships, that's when kids (and adults) try to "mind read" what other people are thinking. They usually come up with the wrong conclusions.

If a relationship feels a bit icky, ask your inner coping coach for the courage to ask yourself questions like:

- "Are you okay?"
- "Is there something I need to say?"

Or any other questions your inner coping coach comes up with. Remember though, it's sometimes not about something you have or have not done, often it's what's going on for the other person and how they are interpreting the world too.

How to improve relationships

There's always room to improve your relationships, including the one with you.

Step one is to always start with honesty.

Step two is become curious about the way you speak and the way you listen. Are you being compassionate and respectful of what people have to say too?

Step three is balance. Make sure you prioritise time for all your relationships.

Step four is to do the best that you can with the skills you have now (knowing there's always room for improvement).

Step five is acceptance. Sometimes mix ups in relationships happen because the other person is going through something, it's not always about you. Keep your communication open and honest and be compassionate as they work through 'their' stuff.

Step six is focus. Set self-rules for screen time, games and social media. Focus less on your attachments to things and gadgets, and more on life and those that you care about and who care about you.

Step seven is kindness. Always speak to yourself and others the way you would like to be spoken to. Become your own best friend too!

Changing relationships

A short final note on relationships. They change, and that's okay.

Relationships will come and go. You might have been really good friends with someone one year at school, then the next year they moved away, or something changed, and you now spend less time with them. But the friendships and connections that matter leave an imprint. They make us a better person because we learned something about ourselves by connecting with that person, animal, plant or thing.

How you deal with changes in relationships

Dealing with change is a coping skill I've mentioned in the book a few times in other chapters. Challenges we face cause our life to change all of the time.

If a relationship changes, listen to how that makes you feel. Communicate honestly with the emotion by calling on your inner coping coach.

Remember how powerful a growth mindset is? It helps you learn and to be open to new ways of looking at the world.

Another big learning that happens when you develop a growth mindset is it helps you arrive at a place deep inside called acceptance.

Acceptance

Acceptance means we become peaceful, compassionate and open about something that happened or is happening. Accepting helps you see how to change yourself to meet the change as it happens. Or it helps you decide not to change, (and that's okay too) as long as you accept the consequence of not changing.

What do you have control of when change happens?

You!

You have control over how you think, your reaction and actions. You have control over the emotions you have as a result of your experiences.

C.O.P.E. FORMULA FOR MAKING THE MOST OF YOUR RELATIONSHIPS	
C = CURIOSITY	Become the CURIOUS detective about your relationships. If something triggers an unhelpful reaction, ask *"What can I learn from this?"*
O = OBSERVER	OBSERVE the balance in your relationships. Do you need to adjust your focus to improve some of your relationships?
P = POSITIVITY	Write your POSITIVE plan to say genuine, nice things to yourself and others. Use this affirmation, *"I choose to let things go."* Or write your own.
E = EXPLORER	EXPLORE other emotions that arise when you experience a change to your relationships. Look for ways to improve.

Make a list of any unkind things you say or think to yourself (or others) if something happens to change a relationship. Ask your inner coping coach what you could say instead

_____

_____

_____

Write a positive visualisation or affirmation about improving the way you cope with changes to your relationships

_____

_____

_____

Remember, as I mentioned in Chapter 7, you get to choose whether you interpret your emotions as helpful or unhelpful. The same goes for your reaction to change in relationships, or when relationships cause upset. These times can be our greatest gift if we have a growth mindset toward them.

This brings you to the final steps of the book. You've been through quite a journey so far, so let's bring it all together in the next chapter and see how far you've come.

Remember, don't cop it! C.O.P.E. with it!

CHAPTER 9

COPE WITH ANYTHING, ANYTIME

Throughout the book, I've talked about lots of different challenges and provided a bunch of coping skills to help you manage better. But the bigger purpose of the book is to show you that you can cope with anything.

Let's expand the skills you've started to learn. The skill of curiously acknowledging feelings like a detective is the best coping skill you'll ever learn. It's the foundation to help you use all the other skills.

Let's learn how you can use that same set of skills for everything now. Rather than getting overwhelmed with emotions that show up as sensations like tightness, or fluttering anxiety in the body or overwhelm in the head, you can learn to manage anything.

You can now use the C.O.P.E. skills to adapt to everything.

How emotions show up

Sometimes you don't recognise emotions because they hide themselves as sensations in your body.

- Have you ever had a sick feeling in your tummy when something new happens that you're a bit scared about?
- Or butterflies in your belly if you're about to compete or go on stage or read in front of the class?

> Sometimes you don't recognise emotions because they hide themselves as sensations in your body.

Adults call those sensations either nervousness or excitement. It depends on whether they interpret the situation as good or bad.

Perhaps you've felt a funny feeling that you can't name, a heaviness in your legs or arms, or a stuck feeling, tingling in your body or even pain somewhere? Often there's an emotion lurking underneath the sensation.

> Often there's an emotion lurking underneath the sensation.

What can you do when emotions become sensations in the body?

1. Be the curious detective to acknowledge how you feel.

As I've already said earlier in the book, these emotions and sensations hold messages for you from your body or from your unconscious mind. When you stop and curiously notice what's happening in your body like a detective, you automatically take your power back to change what's happening.

Most of us want to ignore our feelings if we don't like them. But when you notice them, the most important thing is to be curious and spend time observing them.

2. Imagine your brain is like the control room of your body and your mind is the control room operator, running the entire system that is, YOU!

I think about my body as the house that I live in. My emotions, sensations and thoughts are the doorbell that rings to let me know someone is there.

If you were to use your curious detective to remember your body is your house and you can use your mind to operate the control centre, you can choose to invite your emotions or sensations and thoughts into the control room to talk to the operator (your mind) about how to resolve how you feel. All without hurting anybody or anything.

3. Call your inner team together.

The next step is to call your inner team together, (your coping coach, the control room operator and the curious detective). Spend time in the control room working as a team, adjusting the switches, computer screen and dials that control the way you react. As a team you can reduce tension or other sensations, balance emotions and listen to what those emotions have to say.

You get to work out a plan to resolve the emotion.

> Your inner coping team are cleverer than you think. They'll help you come up with your own solution, or you can pick up this book and open to any C.O.P.E. formula and do the exercises.

Never ignore your emotions, thoughts and sensations, they're nothing to be afraid of. In fact, they have the answers to help you feel better.

Get to know yourself

How does your body react when your emotions show up? Get to know how your body holds feelings for you. Be curious and see if there are patterns.

- When some emotions arise, you might notice your heart races
- Others might cause your heart to feel heavy or somehow broken
- You might get tense in your neck or shoulders
- Your hand might tighten and close
- You might think thoughts are racing in your head or coming from everywhere
- You might have tingling sensations with some emotions or prickly ones with others

There's no right or wrong, everyone does this differently. Your body will have unique ways to tell you what's happening inside with your emotions. That's why it would be useful to spend a few quiet moments calling your 'inner coping team' together in the control room and doing your own curious research on your emotions and sensations.

So, close your eyes, sit with your team and breathe deeply for a few minutes. This is your chance to cope with anything, any emotion, anytime.

C.O.P.E. FORMULA COPE WITH ANYTHING, ANY EMOTION, ANYTIME	
C = CURIOSITY	Become the CURIOUS detective about everything. If you experience a strong sensation when you have an emotion or a thought, stop and call your inner coaching team to the control room. Ask the team which of the coping skills will help you. Or open this book and choose one.
O = OBSERVER	OBSERVE your body and make a list of your emotions, thoughts and sensations. Are there patterns? Consult your inner coping team to work out what those emotions and sensations tell you.
P = POSITIVITY	Use a POSITIVE affirmation each week and repeat it to yourself every time you need some extra support. *"I love and accept me."* Or *"I'm learning to let stuff go."*
E = EXPLORER	EXPLORE other patterns that arise when you don't feel right. You're in control of how you react. Look for ways to move forward and create that better version of yourself.

Make a list of the patterns that come up for you with emotions, thoughts and sensations.

_____

_____

_____

Write a positive affirmation to improve the way you cope. Visualise new reactions to every day challenges so your control centre learns how to react differently from today _____

_____

_____

Remember, as I've mentioned right throughout this book, you get to choose whether you accept your emotions as helpful or unhelpful. You get to choose how you react from today.

You get to be the best version of you. Practice your coping skills daily, don't let anything get past you.

Remember, don't cop it! C.O.P.E. with it!

GLOSSARY OF TERMS

TERM	MEANING
ATTITUDE	The way you think or feel about something or someone. Attitude will influence your actions and response. You can have a variety of attitudes to different things. You can change your attitude if you want to (just like changing a hat).
EMOTIONAL TRIGGERS	An event, or person, or something someone says, or even a sound or smell that triggers you unconsciously to react. For example, a trigger could be an event that makes you suddenly angry and changes the way you behave. Or a time of the year like Christmas that triggers a different reaction.
FORGIVENESS	When you decide to change your feelings and attitude towards what someone did or did not say or do. You let go of negative emotions toward that person, event or thing, and feel peaceful or neutral inside when you think about the person or remember the experience and what was said or done.
GROWTH MINDSET	Being flexible to learn to change. Believing you are in control of your reactions, ability and destiny. Believing and having the skills to accept you can learn and improve from every experience (even the not so good ones). Knowing that it's okay to make mistakes and experience change because you will learn and grow.

TERM	MEANING
INNER COPING | COACHING TEAM	The internal support team you can call upon to help you cope with challenges. Consists of your Inner Coping Coach, your Curious Detective and your Control Room Operator.
PRESSURE	Pressure is external to you. Something that you have no control over.
PROCRASTINATE / PROCRASTINATION	When you delay starting or completing a task. For example, when you have been given a project, or asked to do a chore, but you procrastinate by doing anything else except the task you were given.
REFRAMING	When you think about something from a different angle it can cause you to automatically change how you think or react. After reframing something people often say something like, *"Oh, I hadn't thought of it like that."*
STRESS	When you have created demands and expectations within yourself, but you're unable to deal with them because you don't have the resources or coping skills. For example, if you are given the external pressure of an exam at school, but you feel overwhelmed by it or don't have a plan to study for it until it's too late.

ACKNOWLEDGMENTS

I would like to acknowledge these inspirational, helpful, and encouraging people. In one way or another, you have contributed to the realisation of this book. I am so very grateful.

First of all, I thank that version of 'myself' who gets things done with ease. I am forever grateful. You are a true inner coach, and you have been very patient. I am proud!

An impact on my assessment and evaluation comes from my two sons Christian and Elias. I have watched you both exercise coping skills from the beginning. Not too long-ago Elias told me *"you did something right mum. Christian and I don't feel any complex sadness or anxiety or struggle with the issues that we see others struggling with. Whatever you did, you did good mum.)*

The best bunch of words I have ever received. But let me add they have been raised by a wonderful father and lots of other "mummies" too.

Let's say I practiced the skills that I proposed in this book as my kids were growing. The best thing that I witnessed was my boys faced and felt all challenges without me running to save them. They would then explore their own solutions. And when they made wrong decisions, their mistakes turned into useful (and sometimes not so useful) feedback. My boys became comfortable with making mistakes and growing from them. Lots of credit goes to their school too 'The Scots College'.

The wonderful Maggie Wilde, my publisher (Mind Potential Publishing) showed me how writing this book would be an amazing experience. So, thank you, my ride was smooth. I was supported and the best of me was encouraged. I'm grateful.

And Trish Walker who supported and kept me accountable. Your relationship was more important than you know.

Every step of this book was shared with my amazing friend Fotini Tsilinikos. You were there to help me research and do all that stuff that I don't like to do. Fotini you have offered wonderful encouragement from the first moment that I told you I was thinking about writing this book. You are a blessing in all areas of my life, and I would need another book just to thank you for the millions of things you do for me.

Fay, Monic, Fotini and Rebecca, you were so helpful when I needed stories and ideas from your kids. You asked other kids and parents to help me get the title, the chapters, the cover, the format and all the stuff that was needed to put it all together.

To the parents of Banbury Cottage, Rainbow Cottage, Little Dolphins, and Babyland, you were an instrumental part of my research, thank you.

Catherine Shaw, thank you for your contribution to my Foreword. Positive Living Skills has been an amazing influence on my early learning centres, and my Positive Thinking Clinic. I'm so happy connected beyond this book.

Noni, Tia, Felicia, Manuel, Jay, Dion and Zander, my amazing little people who have given me strength and confidence that I am on the right path. You kids were there to comfort me during my time of sadness, and I will never forget what you mean to me. I thank you for sharing your life stories with me and letting me help you become amazing versions of yourselves. We became great partners. Thanks for trusting me.

Koukla and Beba my little furry animals, thanks for entertaining me and jumping over my laptop as I wrote my chapters. I apologise

ACKNOWLEDGEMENTS

for those times I had to wake you when you were asleep on my keyboard.

Douni and my dad who now live in sunny heaven. You found a spot in my book. You taught me so much and I've paid that forward. May the rainbows shine bright for you.

My immediate and local community who offered me courage and support whilst writing this book. So many of you pre-ordered the book without reading it because you have faith in my work, and you have allowed me to contribute to your kids' lives. You truly do feel like a big wonderful family to me. There is a little of all of you and your kids somewhere in my book.

Finally, as with all that I create and all that I achieve I have always sensed the essence of support surrounding me. It's like an invisible protector of mine. There is nothing more comforting. Thank you, Louis Dounis, it's a good thing I married you, your quiet support for not just this book but for the amazing chapters in our lives. I'm forever quietly grateful. We have so many of our own chapters together. I thank you dearly.

ABOUT THE CONTRIBUTOR

Cath Shaw is the Founder of *Positive Living Skills initiative in Australia.* The goal of the initiative is to prevent mental health problems before they develop and positively impact the growing statistics of mental illness, bullying and violence that drains our communities.

"When we implement a positive, preventative, practical and effective program at an early age, and support children to transition to High School with the skills they need, we also support teachers, families and the wider community." Cath Shaw

The Positive Living Skills programs are implemented in Early Childhood Centres and Primary Schools across Australia. www.positivelivingskills.com.au

ABOUT THE AUTHOR
– AMANDA DOUNIS

Amanda Dounis is the founder and operator of four award-winning Early Learning Centres in the St. George area of Sydney, Australia. She is the Director of the Dounis Group, and founder of The Positive Thinking Clinic.

She has worked in the early childhood industry for over 20 years and is a member of the Mental Health Academy, National Standards Education Authority, the Australian Counselling Association and Australian Hypnotherapy Association.

Amanda is passionate about child development and helping others uncover their inner strengths. She has a Bachelor of Science (Psychology), a Bachelor of Counselling and a Bachelor of Teaching, a Diploma in Professional Counselling, a Diploma in Child Psychology, and a Diploma in Clinical Hypnotherapy and Strategic Psychotherapy.

Amanda is married with two sons, volunteers for the Lifeline suicide crisis call centre and is a marathon runner. She has a unique philosophy when it comes to being busy in a healthy way:

"I find balance by taking some work with me on vacations, and always having vacation time when I'm at home. This attitude has allowed my businesses to flourish and my personal growth to expand." Amanda Dounis

www.positivethinkingclinic.com.au

Amanda's 4 Early Learning Centres:

https://www.stgeorgechildcare.com.au/banbury_cottage

https://www.stgeorgechildcare.com.au/little_dolphins_long_day_care_centre

https://www.stgeorgechildcare.com.au/babyland_child_care_centre

https://www.stgeorgechildcare.com.au/rainbow_cottage_child_care_centre

WHAT OTHERS HAVE TO SAY...

"My kids attended the workshops and have had the best experience... My eldest son has also seen Amanda one on one and words cannot express what she has done for him... Cannot recommend her enough."

Koula Zacharia

"I have sent my 3 children to some of Amanda's workshops and have been really happy with the outcome and information of these workshops and also really impressed that my children have always been eager to go back a 2nd, 3rd, and 4th time."

Monic Taoube, Early Childhood Professional

"Amanda made my daughter feel at ease straight away. She treated her like an individual, not a text book. She helped her become that happy, confident girl that she once was."

Irene Xakiss

"I especially love the kids holiday clinics that Amanda hosts... The clinic covers topics such as sibling rivalry, bullying, homework, organisation, anxiety (amongst others) which have proved invaluable for my family. Every child should attend these clinics!"

Sevasti Tsavaris

WHAT OTHERS HAVE TO SAY

"I have been sending my daughter (preschool age) to the Positive Thinking Clinic with the beautiful Amanda and she absolutely absorbs every positive experience and recalls everything back to her friends and family.

The atmosphere...is peaceful and calming, ... the way Amanda speaks to the children is respectful and inviting, really giving the children the best opportunity to feel connected...."

Maria Smart Early Childhood Teacher

"Amanda has helped my whole family on a range of things over the last year and cannot recommend her enough... My kids can't wait to return after each workshop they do either."

Emma Pace

www.ingramcontent.com/pod-product-compliance
Lightning Source LLC
Chambersburg PA
CBHW070055120526
44588CB00033B/1534